Cowgirl Logic

Its not just about the horses

With love
Sherry Sikstrom
Oct 2018

A collection of poetry by
Sherry Sikstrom

For the wild ones and the cowgirls,
the farmers, the dreamers and the doers.
And for the horses, for without them,
how might our dreams fly?

I was always a little different. When the others were playing dress up, I was petting calves and cats and horses. When the others were baking in their easy bake ovens, I was out watching a calving, or a c section on a cow. Some tried to shoo me away, but grandpa said," if she wants to learn, let her"

I have had a lifelong love of horses and all animals, and my dream as a child was to have my own horse. Every night I came home and counted my babysitting money and bottle money till I could buy my very own horse. And then when I did, we flew!!! In a family that only had quarter horses I came home with an appaloosa!

I was always the "different one" nice enough, but not like the other girls

When I was 17 I moved out 50 miles from the home farm to the "ranch" just me and my horses and dogs" those who thought well of me said "she has a pioneer spirit" those who didn't just looked at me with derision.

Don't get me wrong, I have had a wonderful life, but I was always a little different. At first, I didn't realize I was different, I just thought we were all supposed to follow "our butterflies". Then, I thought maybe I should try to conform, but honestly, I didn't know how. Eventually I figured out what to do to be like the others, and I realized something… I just didn't want to. I loved chasing butterflies and being just who I am, and along the way I found there were a lot of people who loved me just that way also.

A few years ago, I followed a "butterfly" into the world of blogging, then I began to write, quietly and privately at first but then my muse awoke, and I found I simply could not stop writing!

I wrote about joy and hurt, and I wrote about my heart. And to my utter amazement, when I finally had the courage to share it, I found I was not so different after all, many felt the same, or shared my thoughts. With all that support and encouragement, I took a chance and published my first book of poems, "Telling Tails. and then my second "Tails Trails and Campfire stories". I thought then I was done, I had said all I needed to, but as it turns out I still have some things to say!

So, with that, here is Cowgirl Logic. Some thoughts and feelings, heart songs and some points to ponder. Not all the poems are about horses or farming but then again, not all cowgirls are only about that either!

Sometimes they chase cows, and sometimes they chase butterflies!

Metamorphosis

Tired she goes, while on her way
To where she does not know
Builds a cocoon in a quiet place
And waits there all alone
Time does pass
Before you know
And you may pass her by
But magic comes to those who wait
And from there emerged
A butterfly

Just be,
until we can relinquish control of outcomes
we will never truly exist in a moment
for all you can aim an arrow,
once loosed
its flight is unknown
only its direction

Catch up a good horse

Catch up a good horse
Get him saddled and ready
Make sure he's a good one
A fast one and steady

She'll need him to run
And keep steady pace
To outrun the pain
And blow tears from her face

That cowgirls don't cry
Is a story not true
She surely will weep
But she won't show you

She'll let the tears flow
As surely, she must
But if you should see
She will claim it is dust

But alone with her horse
On a wide open plain
She'll soak up her tears
In his coat and his mane

As tough as she seems
She is tender inside
So, catch up a good horse
And just let her ride

In the eyes of a horse,
you may find your story,
your heart, and your truth.
You need only the courage to look

It's not that I didn't love you

It's not that I didn't try
if you could see how hard it is
to say this last goodbye
I always saw the best in you
but now I see the rest of you
too tired to stand and hold my ground
it's time to turn my life around
it's not that I don't love you
I've said that all before
it's not that I don't love you
it's just I love me more

Prairie Winter

When winter comes to us out here
it comes without much warning
you go to sleep in autumn's glow
and wake to find it storming
from the warm sun's glow
before you know
gone is all the grass
be careful friend
around the bend
you could fall upon your
…
Ask anyone
the north they are from
if they would trade this season
most will say no
they will never go
and each one has their reason

Optimism for the modern girl,
when you wake up and realize your
"fairytale ending" really,
is a broken pumpkin,
a missing shoe and a torn party dress.
Your first thoughts are
"that was fun, let's have pie!"

A Two Track Road

A two track Road
from here to where
Where is it going
Why do I care
Will it lead to adventure?
or places unseen
rolling hills
or fields of green
or something quite different
of quiet and peace
somewhere with water
with ducks and with geese
or a place truly fearsome
with ferocious beasts
I will go where it goes
as long as I roam
or I might turn around
and
let it take me home

Maybe in Mexico

Maybe in Mexico
I'll finally find
a little quiet
and some peace of mind
the sun and the sea
for just a few days
we'll recharge my soul
in myriad ways
maybe in Mexico
maybe this time
I'll just lay on a beach
and try to unwind
or go up in the jungle
up in the hills
find me an adventure
find me some thrills
or maybe in Mexico
all I will find
is lots of tequila
and a whole bunch of lime

Whispers from beyond

On a cool autumn morning
just past the dawn
with the sun breaking through
and the mist not yet gone
I open my eyes
to the start of the day
the webs of the night
still fading away
in my wondering eyes
now comes into view
the magical creatures
and loves that I knew
a glimpse for a flash
and then they are gone
yet to me this proof
that the love does live on
in that magical time
in the breaking of day
they visit with me
but are not meant to stay
a fleeting gift
not one to hold on
just food for my soul
and my heart to stay strong

Love the ugly duckling
before she becomes a swan
the one who is different
before she gives in and conforms
the shy and the fearful
the quietly courageous
in the lonely
the ones who are not
bright shining stars every day
better a simple candle
to warm and guide you
should you choose to let them

Living Green

In the war for the environments
there are some forgotten soldiers
they are not heard, or seen that much
don't stand on other shoulders
they don't yell out loud or holler foul
not like those TV charmers
their armor is their coveralls
I'm talking about farmers

Reduce, reuse, recycle man?
The farmer he does all he can
rebuilds a part he won't replace
and never does he waste on space
not one to tell you how to live
you could learn from his advice
after all, he has learned
to use the groceries twice

No matter how frivolous, or silly you find a person to be
remember, they are just as much a miracle as the stars in the sky. And you should take them
just as seriously as you take yourself.
You never know when that one person you least expect will change the world.
So close your mouth for a time and listen, even to what you don't want to hear.

The yard sale

Right time right place
they will come on in droves
looking for bargains
on treasure and clothes
dishes and trinkets
not meant to be kept
or old wooden cradles
where dollies have slept
a huge rototiller
now rusted and old
but back in the day
a garden it rolled
it still works just fine
it just isn't pretty
but if you don't garden
there it sits
what a pity
spare saddles and bridles
not used anymore
will give you a fine deal
far less than the store
now don't you go thinking
these items are trash
they're somebody's treasure
and somebody's cash

Carry-on coyote

Summer winter spring and fall
we often hear the coyote call
at end of day in fading light
they begin their music of the night
and often lonesome eerie sound
reminds us that they are around
they are a lovely creature true
but oh, the damage they can do
a peaceful life I try to live
but the coyote needs to learn to give
a wider berth around the farm
no, we aren't fooled by your charm
so, carry on along your way
there is no place for you to stay
the stock here is mine to tend
and should you linger
you will find your end

Daylight savings

Springing forward falling back
sleep is lost to the attack
of the ringing of a loud alarm
as chores need doing
all over the farm

Day is day
and night, is night
when will they learn
you cannot save light
oh well it is
as it will be
not much to be done
and as for me
I'll wake when I do
and sleep when I should
and saving time
will do no good

Picture

I took your picture off the wall
as though you were never here,
at all
yet I close my eyes and see your face
ever present in this place
I took the picture down you see
because it made me cry
in the next moments though
my heart begged me to know why
I wanted for a time
to hide away from my tears
I thought if I couldn't see you
I could forget all those years
the lessons, laughter, love and time
the memories, that are just mine

I thought if I could forget
I could let go the pain
but then, only emptiness would remain

I hung your picture on the wall
there it will always stay
I remember the love
I let the tears fall
and I hung your picture on the wall

Girls like me

Girls like me
our souls they are old
Judge us if you must
we will remain bold
determined and stubborn
and tough as all hell
we do what we do
and we do it damn well
sarcastic and feisty
yeah, we live openhearted
you don't have to love us
but when we are parted
you will find looking back
you might finally see
that just what you needed
was a girl just like me

For the girls

Who is this woman
who is this girl
she's somebody's daughter
she's somebody's world
she is meek she is fierce
she is shy she is bold
a she wolf or angel
she is young
she is old
she's not just her looks
or the hue of her skin
she is special
her magic
comes from within
who is that woman
who is that girl
she's somebody's daughter
she's somebody's world

On a good day
On a good day I can do anything
just like I could before
on other days I try and fail
as pain begins to soar
it comes and goes
from time to time
for no rhyme or any reason
not from overwork or stress
the weather or the season
not from something I have done wrong
I did not rest too little
or too long
day-to-day I walk a line
but if you ask I am just fine
because I am overall
the pain is part of me that's small
it does not change my heart or mind
it is simply not how I am defined
I am not alone
nor first to feel
this pain that is so very real
judgment comes now and again
from those who cannot see
what's going on inside
or
how those words hurt me
yet on a good day
I can do anything
just like I could before

Shadows cannot exist in total darkness
there must be some light
look for the light
not the darkness
search for the joy
believe the best in life
and in people
after all
a diamond is just a rock
until someone polishes it
with the belief it can be beautiful

For the wild ones

Before we were hurt
before we were scared
when we took life flat out
just because we were dared
jumped into the water
not thinking disaster
the current was strong
so, we just swam faster

The horses we rode
the stories we told
the chances were taking
we were fearless and bold

Up till the wee hours
always home late
chores done at six
at work by eight

So why did we stop
do we really get smarter?
or was keeping that pace
just getting harder

Now don't you worry
she is still there inside
a little bit tired
but she hasn't died

once in a while
if the timing is right
she will howl at the moon
and dance through the night

So, here's to the wild ones
wherever they are
I'll drink a toast to us
out under the stars

Life isn't always beautiful
sometimes it is messy
wonderfully so
we are not all of us meant to be stars
some of us are meant to be stargazers
but always there is music
in the song on the wind,
the song in your heart, and
the birds and the grasses
if your heart is listening
also, always there is magic
if you're willing to see

Dance with your darlin'

Dance with your darlin'
out under a star
a romance not found
in night club or bar
let the moon shine
under wide open skies
the light of the stars
reflect
love in your eyes
laugh dance and twirl
one another around
just you two together
along with the sound
of nature's sweet music
and the love you have found
once in a while
wherever you are
dance with your darlin'
out under a star

I am not afraid of the dark
yet I search for the light
loneliness doesn't come from being alone
it can be a dragon
fueled by self-loathing and doubts
being alone takes courage, and grit
and the willingness to face
who you really are
not just who you are pretending to be
I would take a million nights alone
with my authenticity
over an hour
in a crowd of pretenders

For the lost ones

For the lost and weary souls
in the great somewhere out there
who wish with all their tender hearts
to have someone to care
hold on dear friends
and don't give up
as care we do
and search for you
our candles burning brightly
we pray our paths soon shall cross
and we may hold you tightly

Every day brings the opportunity to grow and to thrive
or to wallow and to become stale
to nurture and raise others up,
or to judge and put down
to go with the crowd and be who the world thinks you should,
or to stand alone and be authentic
the choice isn't always easy or popular
but the results are defining

There is a special energy in a rainstorm
if you are quiet in
yourself you can feel the renewal
like you are on the edge
of something wonderful
then comes the rainbow

A salute to Captain Mark

You should have seen me
when I was young
a sight to behold
and oh, could I run
the fast cars
and fast living
they all played a role
the times I remember
now that I am old
don't pity me now
that I am old, and I'm bent
I still have my memories
of times I have spent
and if you look closely
there still shows a spark
of then and of now
all hail Captain Mark

In matters of love we cannot demand love meet our needs
rather we love simply, and without condition
the love we are seeking can be a reflection of the love we send out
we don't after all, tell the sun at what intensity it must shine

Let go the rope

Sometimes we hold fast to anger and pain
to the hurt and the loss are all that remain
the need to hold on is futile of course
you're as likely to hold back a runaway horse
you can't push back a train alone on a track
nor can you heal while on the attack
better to choose love and to choose hope
you see sometimes
you must
let go the rope

I tried

I tried, I want you to know I tried
I gave it my best
but I can't
as the tears come now
it becomes plain
when I said I was okay I lied
too much too close to soon
it will be better in time I am sure
but for now, I need rest
my soul my heart my mind need a break
I have faced all that I can endure
find me in a place of peace
a place where my heart can release
the pain and the fear
the unshed tears
for there I will quietly rest
in a place that heals me the best
for a moment for an hour for a day
then I will return recovered
and back into the fray

Holiday countdown

Bright red ears and windblown hair
yup it's getting fresh out there
the north wind blows with all its might
and temperatures drop overnight
and now we go to frozen noses
cheeks as red as summer's roses
as winter gives its bitter nip
it makes me want to take a trip
to places where the sun is shining
tropical drinks and outdoor dining
I love it here don't get me wrong
but some days the winter seems so long
as I come in at end of day
and get my dinner underway
I get a good warm fire burning
while in my heart for spring I'm yearning
but I can take it this I know
it's three more weeks to Mexico

A mother

Whether she is near or far
or in the light of a bright star
your mother is with you always
in the things that you do
the traditions you knew
and the life that you live
all of your days
the lessons you learned
and the grey hairs she earned
those moments she held on too tightly
the way that she smiled
with love for her child
and worried and prayed for you nightly
in the way you keep house
or run from a mouse
she is there in so much of who you are
she is there in your eyes
in the way that you try
and all the things that you do
the tilt of your head
the words that she said
will forever keep her so close
this woman whose love help to form you
with the sun on your face
remember her grace
and let her great love still warm you

Just like your mother

You're just like your mother! said in a derisive tone
I'm not you reply, I am me, on my own
I'm nothing like her, we say in our youth
we ignore all those signs blind to see truth
mother, beautiful tenacious and strong
loved us in her way her entire life long
in youth we won't see the parts we are afraid of
but maturity brings understanding and love
mothers aren't perfect, and nor should they be
they are simply women, like you and like me
blessed with the gift of their beautiful child
when they were young,
they were, fearless and wild
they played, and they loved
and they made some mistakes
they grew they matured
and learned what it takes
to put the children first
at their best and their worst
when you think of your mother
as boring or silly
she's something quite different
remember
she's really someone like you
she learns that she goes
a daughter, a sister, a beautiful rose
you're just like your mother
I reply no, you are wrong
I'm not like her yet
I'm just not that strong

For an Auntie's girl

I cried the day I met you
and heard your tiny cry
the day I became your Auntie
I knew one day you'd fly
and fly you did my beauty
took on life full force
not one to just go with the flow
you mapped your very own course
Time has passed so quickly
truly it has flown
and here you are just starting
a family of your own
what wondrous days lie ahead for you
a time of joy and glory
I want to say how proud I am
and blessed
to share in your story

A little bird story

The raven and crows chuckled out their delight.
Staying just out of reach
but not out of sight.
They would laugh and tease
A secret they knew.
a secret I asked?
No, we won't tell you.
An eagle soared high
and the grouse started drumming
what's it all about?
There's a miracle coming.
A single white feather drifted to the ground
the message it brought
there's hope to be found.
Excitement and joy in all far and near
the patient said wise owl,
the time's not yet here
then suddenly, magically
on a morning so bright
The chickadees sang their song of delight.
And what did the little birds sing on that day?
That Birdie Patricia had come home to stay

Forever with us

We will set a special place at our table
and raise a glass up to you
we know you'd be here if you were able
but that you cannot do

But as we give thanks and gather around
in our hearts you will be found
for though we know that now you rest
safe in God's love and grace
forever you shall be our guest
though we may not see your face

We will think of you, give thanks and pray
And know we will meet again someday

But until that day comes to pass
we will set you a place
and raise up a glass
in our hearts and our prayers
we will hold you dear
forever there
keep you near

War

Not every battle
explodes with guns
and violence
sometimes weapons are
words, darkness, and silence
defenseless alone,
with nowhere to hide
desperate for safety
a warm hand to guide
how can this happen
in a world so enlightened
that we are left as lost children
alone and so frightened
can it be changed?
can we be saved?
or are we doomed to this fear
alone yet enslaved?
Throw open the door
Let in the light
leave no weary soul
alone in the night
let your words
be used wisely
not cutting like knives
and remember the value
that exists in our lives
let your heart be made peaceful
your smile like the way
and prayer bring us healing
in each coming day

There is a difference between knowing someone and understanding them, while you may know all about them, and their strengths and weaknesses understanding is knowing why you should never use those weaknesses against them.

Why

Mother Earth and Father Sky
I want to know
to ask you why
why lightning flashes
why thunder rolls
tell me why
I want to know
what makes the sun
brown my skin
where rivers end
and seas begin
what makes the moon
light the night
why some stars are dim
and some are bright
what built the mountains
in all their glory
please sit with me
and tell the story
Mother Earth and Father Sky
the birds, the bears, the wild ones, and I,
promise to listen
and keep asking why

Here's to the horses

Here's the horses that taught us our stuff
of patience compassion and how to be tough
how to sit and to listen and how to eat dust
to be quiet and gentle and how just to trust
the biters the kickers the ones that could buck
the reason all cowgirls need a really good truck
beautiful rides on wide-open trails
and hours of fencing with a fistful of nails
miles of vet wrap we have in our stores
potions and ointments for wounds and for sores
the hours of cold and sleepless long nights
till signs of a colic are again put to rights
and just when we think we are so very smart
along comes the one who makes us a dirt dart
every horse shares new things in its turn
and shows us we have still so much to learn
so, here's the horses that taught us our stuff
as much as they taught us it's still not enough

What Appaloosas teach us
It's okay to be different
maybe even better
wear your hair anyway you like
and if you don't have much that's okay
being bright and thinking, not blindly following the crowd
and being a leader is good
some folks will like you for it but that's not actually your problem
celebrate grey hairs
be exactly who you are there is nobody exactly like you
confidence builds competence
in a world of solid colors celebrate your spots
be yourself, it's a tough act to follow

When speaking of love
I say heart over heels because when it comes to matters of the heart
the head has no say.

A bridge to heaven

If there could be a bridge somehow
from here to heaven's gate
you know that we would rush right out
and cross it just to wait
for a chance to glimpse your smile
or sit and talk to you a while
to say the thank you that we need to say
for your wisdom and love
and your quiet way
your gentle heart and sparkling eyes
will ever be missed as we say our goodbyes
a bridge from here to heaven
would be a daunting task
but if it could be built somehow
you would be the man to ask

Dedicated in loving memory to my father-in-law Larry Sikstrom

I thought I met an angel once

I thought I met an angel once
she opened heart and home
full of light and love and grace
no one left to feel alone
a lady of class and dignity
she showed just what that means
a lady is what you are inside
and ladies can wear jeans
a fierce and loyal mama bear
when life its trials did bring
yet tenderly she cared for all
beneath her gentle wing
years they passed time flies away
nothing goes just as planned
the sad farewell arrives one day
and is so hard to understand
but the wondrous thing about angels is
they never leave your hearts
all need to be done is remember them
and you truly never part
I thought I met an angel once
oh, many years ago
and the blessing that that angel was
I believe that all should know

For the little ones

Hold fast onto those memories
the pageants and the spelling bees
the first steps and the first time you heard
I love you, those three precious words
hold those times close in your heart
as you watch the young life start
those days too quickly slip away
as they grow and change and make their way
too bright and exciting lives
they might stumble
some will fall
just like we did ourselves
be slow to judge
and quick to love they are who they will be

Hitch your wagon to a star
not mine, mind you, she's a bit of a bronc
and you never know
where she might take you.

I bid you farewell for now, but maybe not forever. I have more adventures to live, more stories to enjoy, and more butterflies to chase.

Many thanks to all who have supported me in my journey and who continue to support me going forward. And a special acknowledgement to my niece Deanna Scott for her beautiful pictures of Johnny Handsome and I. Those pictures on that day were a great reminder that our time is not promised, and we must celebrate each moment. I will continue my love affair with all of God's creatures and leave you with a line from one of my favorite hymns.

"All things Bright and beautiful
All creatures great and small.
All things wise and wonderful
the Lord God made them all"

Made in the USA
San Bernardino, CA
25 September 2018